GENERATIVE AI FRAMEWORKS

Contents

Part I: Foundations of Generative AI

Chapter 1: Introduction to Generative AI

Welcome to the fascinating world of Generative AI (GenAI)! This chapter will introduce you to the core concepts of GenAI, explore its applications across various fields, and delve into its historical evolution.

1.1 What is Generative AI?

Imagine a world where machines can not only understand and respond to information, but also create entirely new content. This is the essence of Generative AI. GenAI refers to a branch of Artificial Intelligence (AI) focused on developing algorithms that can generate novel and creative text, code, images, music, and other types of data.

1.2 Core Concepts of GenAI

- **Learning from Data:** GenAI models are trained on massive datasets of existing content. This training allows them to identify patterns and relationships within the data.

- **Generating New Content:** Once trained, GenAI models can use their knowledge of the data to

produce entirely new outputs. This could be
anything from a poem inspired by famous works
of literature to a realistic image of an animal
that doesn't actually exist.

- **Diverse Applications:** The potential applications
  of GenAI are vast and ever-growing. We'll
  explore some specific examples in the next
  section.

1.3 Applications of GenAI across Various Fields

GenAI is transforming numerous industries with its
ability to automate tasks, enhance creativity, and
personalize experiences. Here are a few examples:

- **Creative Content Generation:**

- Writers can use GenAI to overcome writer's block or generate new ideas for stories and poems.
- Musicians can create unique melodies and song lyrics with the help of GenAI.
- Graphic designers can leverage GenAI to produce new design concepts and variations.

- **Marketing and Advertising:**
  - GenAI can be used to personalize marketing messages and create targeted advertising campaigns.
  - Chatbots powered by GenAI can provide customer service and answer product inquiries.

- **Drug Discovery and Material Science:**

  - GenAI can analyze vast amounts of scientific data to accelerate drug discovery and materials development.

  - Researchers can use GenAI to generate new molecule structures with desired properties.

- **Education and Training:**

  - GenAI can personalize learning experiences for students by adapting to their individual needs and pace.

  - Interactive learning tools powered by GenAI can create engaging and immersive educational experiences.

1.4 Historical Perspective on the Evolution of GenAI

The field of GenAI has seen significant advancements in recent years. Here are some key milestones:

- **Early AI Models (1950s-1980s):** Early attempts at AI focused on rule-based systems and symbolic logic. These models had limited capabilities in generating creative content.

- **Statistical Machine Learning (1990s-2000s):** Statistical machine learning algorithms emerged, allowing models to learn from data patterns. This led to some advancements in text generation.

- **Deep Learning and the Rise of LLMs (2010s-Present):** The development of deep learning architectures, particularly transformers, revolutionized GenAI. Large Language Models

(LLMs) trained on massive datasets achieved

unprecedented levels of performance in

generating text, code, and other content.

This concludes Chapter 1. The next chapter will delve

deeper into the workings of LLMs, the backbone of

many GenAI applications.

Chapter 2: Unveiling Large Language Models (LLMs)

Large Language Models (LLMs) are the backbone of Generative AI (GenAI). In this chapter, we'll delve into their inner workings, explore how they're trained, and discover their strengths and limitations in various tasks.

2.1 Understanding the Concept of LLMs and their Role in GenAI

Imagine a computer program that can not only understand human language but also use it to generate creative text formats, translate languages, write different kinds of creative content, and answer your questions in an informative way. That's the power of LLMs!

- **LLMs Explained:**
  - LLMs are complex algorithms trained on massive amounts of text data (books, articles, code, webpages).
  - By analyzing these vast datasets, LLMs learn the patterns and relationships between words, allowing them to generate similar text formats and respond to prompts and questions in a human-like way.

- **The Role of LLMs in GenAI:**
  - LLMs are the core technology behind many GenAI applications.

- They provide the foundation for tasks like:
    - Text generation: Creating poems, scripts, musical pieces, and other creative text formats.
    - Machine translation: Translating languages with greater accuracy and fluency.
    - Question answering: Answering your questions in an informative way, even if they are open ended, challenging, or strange.
    - Chatbots and virtual assistants: Powering chatbots that can engage in conversations and virtual

assistants that can perform tasks

based on your instructions.

2.2 Exploring the Training Process and Data

Requirements for LLMs

Training an LLM is no small feat. Here's a glimpse into

the process:

- **Data Collection:** The first step involves

  gathering massive amounts of text data. This

  data can come from books, articles, code

repositories, webpages, and other sources. The quality and diversity of the data are crucial for the LLM's performance.

- **Data Preprocessing:** The raw data needs to be cleaned and formatted for the LLM to understand it. This might involve removing irrelevant information, correcting errors, and ensuring consistency.

- **Model Selection and Training:** A specific LLM architecture (e.g., transformers) is chosen, and the model is trained on the prepared data. This training process can take days or even weeks on powerful computer systems.

- **Fine-Tuning:** Once trained, the LLM can be fine-tuned for specific tasks. For example, an LLM trained for translation might be further trained on a dataset of translated documents to improve its accuracy in a particular language pair.

2.3 Strengths and Limitations of LLMs in Various Tasks

LLMs offer a range of capabilities, but it's important to understand their limitations as well.

- **Strengths of LLMs:**
    - **Text Generation:** LLMs excel at generating different creative text formats, often producing human-quality writing.
        - **Case Study:** An advertising agency uses an LLM to generate creative

taglines for their client's marketing

campaign. The LLM's ability to

produce a variety of options helps

the agency brainstorm new ideas.

- **Machine Translation:** LLMs can translate

languages with greater accuracy and

fluency compared to traditional machine

translation methods.

  - **Use Case:** Travelers can use an LLM-

  powered translation app to have

  real-time conversations with locals

  while abroad, breaking down

  language barriers.

- **Question Answering:** LLMs can access and

process information from vast amounts of

data to answer your questions in an informative way, even if they are open ended, challenging, or strange.

- **Example:** A student studying for an exam can use an LLM to answer complex questions about a particular topic, helping them gain a deeper understanding of the subject.

- **Limitations of LLMs:**

  - **Lack of Common Sense Reasoning:** LLMs can struggle with tasks that require common sense reasoning or understanding the context of a situation.

    - For instance, an LLM asked to write a story about a robot chef might create a nonsensical scenario where the robot uses a blender to cook a steak.

- Bias from Training Data: LLMs can inherit biases from the data they are trained on. It's crucial to ensure training data is diverse and unbiased to avoid perpetuating stereotypes or misinformation.

- Limited Ability to Explain Reasoning: Understanding how LLMs arrive at their outputs can be challenging. This lack of transparency is an ongoing area of research.

Conclusion

Large Language Models are powerful tools with the

potential to revolutionize various aspects of our lives.

By understanding their strengths and limitations, we

can leverage LLMs for creative endeavors, enhance

communication, and access information more

effectively. As research continues, LLMs will likely

become even more sophisticated, opening

Part II: Pioneering Generative AI Frameworks

Part II dives into some of the groundbreaking

frameworks that have shaped the landscape of

Generative AI (GenAI). Here, we'll explore three

prominent models: GPT, Gemini (assuming it refers to

the factual language model you are based on), and

LaMDA.

Advanced Architectures in Generative AI

Generative AI has made significant strides with the development of architectures that enable machines to create content as complex as human-made works. At the forefront of these advancements are models like Generative Adversarial Networks (GANs), Variational

Autoencoders (VAEs), and transformers such as GPT,

which drive innovation in various fields including

image synthesis, text generation, and even

multimodal applications. The underlying principle of

generative AI is to teach machines how to understand

and replicate complex data distributions, enabling

them to produce novel outputs that are

indistinguishable from original human-created

content.

GANs have become one of the most influential

innovations in generative AI. A GAN consists of two

neural networks: the generator and the discriminator.

The generator's job is to produce new data points,

while the discriminator attempts to distinguish

between real and fake data. The adversarial process that ensues between these two components leads to progressively better outputs. Over time, GANs have been adapted for numerous tasks, from generating photorealistic images (StyleGAN) to synthesizing text and video (Text-to-Image GANs, Video GANs). However, the challenge with GANs is ensuring that the generator produces diverse outputs without falling into common pitfalls like mode collapse, where the generator produces similar outputs repeatedly.

On the other hand, Variational Autoencoders (VAEs) use a different approach to generate new data. VAEs are based on probabilistic modeling and are particularly powerful for data compression and generation. The encoder maps input data into a latent space, which is essentially a compressed representation of the data, while the decoder reconstructs the original data from this latent representation. The generative power of VAEs lies in their ability to sample from the latent space and generate new data that shares the characteristics of the original data. VAEs, while not always as sharp or realistic as GAN-generated images, are often used for tasks where interpretability and control over the generated outputs are crucial.

Transformers, initially designed for sequence-to-sequence tasks like machine translation, have revolutionized natural language processing and are now being adapted for generative tasks. Models like

GPT-4 (Generative Pretrained Transformer) and

DALL·E (for image generation) use transformer

architectures to process and generate coherent

sequences of text or images. Unlike GANs and VAEs,

transformers are based on attention mechanisms that

allow the model to weigh the importance of different

words or pixels when generating new content. This

enables transformers to generate highly coherent and

contextually accurate outputs, making them the go-to

choice for tasks like text generation, translation,

summarization, and even generating images from text

prompts.

The evolution of these generative frameworks marks a significant shift in the way AI systems approach content creation, but each of these architectures comes with its own set of challenges and trade-offs. GANs are notorious for their training instability, VAEs can produce blurry outputs, and transformers, while powerful, require vast computational resources and large-scale datasets to achieve state-of-the-art performance.

Model Optimization and Efficiency in Generative AI

As the complexity of generative models continues to increase, optimizing these models for both performance and efficiency has become a critical area of focus. A key challenge in generative AI is balancing the accuracy of the model with computational cost. The sheer size of models like GPT-4 or DALL·E demands significant computing power, which is often unaffordable for many organizations. Therefore, a growing focus has been placed on techniques like model pruning, quantization, knowledge distillation, and transfer learning to make these models more accessible and efficient.

Model pruning is the process of removing weights from a trained model that contribute little to its output, effectively reducing the model's size and computational demands without sacrificing accuracy. This is particularly important for deploying generative models in resource-constrained environments, such as on edge devices or mobile platforms. By removing redundant parameters, pruning can reduce the size of models by orders of magnitude while maintaining performance levels close to the full model.

Quantization further enhances the efficiency of generative AI models by reducing the precision of the model's weights. Instead of storing parameters as high-precision floating-point numbers, they can be represented with lower precision, significantly reducing memory and computational requirements. Quantization techniques have become increasingly sophisticated, allowing models to be fine-tuned for deployment in environments with limited resources, such as smartphones or embedded systems.

Knowledge distillation is another technique used to make large generative models more efficient. In this approach, a smaller "student" model is trained to mimic the behavior of a much larger "teacher" model. The goal is for the student model to approximate the performance of the teacher while using far fewer computational resources. This method has been shown to work effectively for generative models, particularly in scenarios where high performance is needed but resources are limited.

Transfer learning also plays an essential role in optimizing generative AI models. In this approach, a model that has already been trained on a large

dataset for a specific task is fine-tuned on a smaller

dataset tailored to the task at hand. This allows

developers to leverage the powerful representations

learned by the model during pretraining, significantly

reducing the time and resources required to train a

new model from scratch.

Furthermore, the efficient deployment of generative

AI models requires optimizing their architecture for

parallelism, both at the level of data and computation.

Distributed training frameworks, such as Horovod and

DeepSpeed, allow large-scale models to be trained

across multiple GPUs or even clusters of machines,

speeding up the training process and making it

feasible to train more complex models. The use of specialized hardware like Tensor Processing Units (TPUs) and Graphics Processing Units (GPUs) further accelerates the training and inference times for generative models, enabling the real-time generation of content across a variety of applications.

Multimodal Generative AI: Bridging the Gap Between Text, Image, and Audio

In the last few years, multimodal generative AI has emerged as a powerful approach for creating models that can simultaneously handle multiple types of data, such as text, images, and audio. These models are able to generate content that involves multiple modalities, such as generating images from textual descriptions or composing music based on written prompts. The integration of multiple data types opens up new possibilities for creative AI applications, ranging from interactive media and art to advanced natural language processing tasks.

One of the most notable examples of multimodal AI is DALL·E, a transformer-based model that generates images from textual descriptions. DALL·E leverages the power of large-scale transformers to understand the relationship between text and visual content. The model is trained on vast datasets that include both images and their corresponding textual descriptions, learning how to map between the two modalities. This ability to generate images from text is a significant leap forward in generative AI, enabling the creation of highly specific and imaginative visuals that previously would have required manual design.

Another prominent example is CLIP (Contrastive Language-Image Pretraining), which is designed to connect images with textual descriptions in a shared latent space. CLIP can understand and relate concepts across modalities, allowing it to perform tasks like zero-shot image classification and image generation from text prompts. By training on a large corpus of both images and textual descriptions, CLIP enables AI systems to generate more contextually accurate and semantically rich outputs.

The integration of audio with text and image generation is also a growing area within multimodal AI. For instance, models like Jukedeck and OpenAI's MuseNet focus on generating music based on textual prompts or even creating sound effects that complement visuals in video content. These models combine techniques from both the generative models used in image and text synthesis and extend them to audio, resulting in the ability to generate cohesive, multimodal experiences.

Multimodal generative AI has numerous applications in creative fields like gaming, entertainment, advertising, and education. By combining the power of text, image, and audio generation, these models provide unprecedented control over the creative process, allowing for the generation of fully immersive and interactive content. The challenge, however, lies in maintaining coherence and quality across different modalities, as the interaction between modalities introduces additional complexity in both training and inference.

Generative AI in Healthcare: Transforming Diagnostics and Drug Discovery

Generative AI is finding transformative applications in healthcare, particularly in the fields of medical diagnostics and drug discovery. These applications leverage the ability of generative models to create novel data that can complement or simulate real-world scenarios, accelerating innovation and decision-making in healthcare.

In medical diagnostics, generative AI models like GANs and VAEs have been used to generate synthetic medical images, such as X-rays, MRIs, and CT scans. These models can generate high-quality, realistic images that are indistinguishable from real patient data, allowing them to be used for training diagnostic models in situations where data is limited. This is especially valuable in cases where patient data is scarce or difficult to obtain, such as for rare diseases or in underserved areas.

Generative models are also used in drug discovery, where they are employed to generate novel molecular structures that have the potential to interact with specific biological targets. By training on large datasets of molecular information, generative models can predict the properties of molecules that have not yet been synthesized, enabling researchers to explore vast chemical spaces and identify promising candidates for drug development. These models have the potential to drastically reduce the time and cost involved in drug discovery, which traditionally requires extensive experimentation and trial-and-error testing.

Moreover, generative models can be used to simulate biological processes, allowing researchers to explore complex interactions between proteins, genes, and other biomolecules. By generating realistic simulations of these processes, AI can provide insights into disease mechanisms and help researchers design better treatments or interventions.

Despite the promise of generative AI in healthcare, challenges remain in terms of model interpretability, regulatory approval, and the integration of AI-generated content into clinical workflows. Nonetheless, the potential for generative AI to revolutionize the healthcare industry is vast, offering the possibility of more accurate diagnostics, faster drug discovery, and personalized medicine.

Ethical Considerations in Generative AI: Navigating the Future

As generative AI continues to evolve, it is crucial to address the ethical challenges associated with its deployment. The ability of AI to create content that mimics human works raises concerns about authenticity, ownership, bias, and potential misuse. One of the primary ethical concerns is the generation of deepfakes—highly realistic but fake media, such as images, videos, and audio—used for malicious purposes, including misinformation and manipulation.

To mitigate the risks associated with deepfakes and other harmful uses of generative AI, several approaches are being explored, including the development of AI tools to detect and flag synthetic media. Researchers are also investigating methods to trace the provenance of generated content, allowing users to verify whether content has been generated by an AI model or created by humans.

Another significant ethical issue is the potential for bias in generative models. Since these models are trained on large datasets, any biases present in the data can be learned and perpetuated by the model. For example, a text-generating model trained on biased data might produce harmful or discriminatory outputs, while an image generation model could reinforce harmful stereotypes. Addressing these biases requires careful attention to the data used for training, as well as the implementation of techniques like fairness auditing and adversarial testing to ensure that AI models produce equitable outcomes.

Generative AI also raises questions about intellectual property and ownership. If an AI model generates an image, a piece of music, or a written work, who owns the rights to that content? This question is particularly important as AI systems become more autonomous and capable of producing novel works. Legal frameworks around intellectual property will need to evolve to account for the contributions of AI in creative processes, ensuring that creators, whether human or machine, are fairly compensated for their work.

As generative AI becomes more integrated into society, it is essential to develop policies and best practices that ensure its ethical use. This includes fostering transparency in AI systems, ensuring accountability for AI-generated content, and promoting diversity and inclusivity in the development of generative models. Ultimately, ethical considerations will play a pivotal role in shaping the future of generative AI and its impact on society.

Advanced Architectures in Generative AI

Generative AI has witnessed transformative advancements over the past few years, with innovative architectures driving the field's rapid evolution. Among the most groundbreaking approaches are Generative Adversarial Networks (GANs), Variational Autoencoders (VAEs), and Transformer models. Each of these architectures introduces unique methodologies for generating new, high-quality data, ranging from images and text to audio and video. The core objective behind these generative frameworks is to teach machines to produce data that mimics the characteristics of real-world data, whether it be visual content, language, or other forms of creative output.

GANs have quickly become the dominant architecture in generative AI, thanks to their ability to create incredibly realistic images, videos, and even sound. GANs consist of two neural networks— a generator and a discriminator— which engage in a competitive process where the generator learns to create realistic data while the discriminator attempts to distinguish between real and fake data. This adversarial process improves the generator's ability to produce high-fidelity outputs over time, resulting in impressive achievements like realistic deepfakes, synthetic art, and even text-to-image generation. While GANs can produce visually stunning results, they are not without challenges. One significant hurdle is training instability, which can lead to issues like mode collapse, where the generator produces similar outputs without diversity. Despite these challenges, GANs remain a cornerstone of generative AI applications.

In contrast, VAEs offer a probabilistic approach to data generation. Rather than relying on adversarial training, VAEs utilize an encoder-decoder framework. The encoder maps input data into a compressed latent space, and the decoder reconstructs the original data. This probabilistic approach allows VAEs to generate new data by sampling from the latent space. While the outputs of VAEs tend to be less sharp and detailed compared to GAN-generated content, their ability to control and interpret the latent space makes them valuable in applications like anomaly detection, semi-supervised learning, and image generation. Furthermore, VAEs are known for their stable training dynamics, making them an attractive alternative in certain scenarios where GANs struggle.

Transformer models, originally designed for natural language processing tasks, have recently revolutionized the field of generative AI. Models like GPT (Generative Pretrained Transformer) and DALL-E have demonstrated impressive results in generating text and images, respectively. Transformers operate by learning to predict the next token in a sequence based on context, using self-attention mechanisms to weigh the importance of different parts of the input data. This architecture has proven highly effective in generating coherent and contextually appropriate sequences, making it ideal for tasks like text generation, translation, and summarization. Moreover, the transferability of transformer-based models to various domains, including image and music generation, showcases their versatility and adaptability. However, one limitation of transformer models is the computational expense associated with training large-scale models, which requires substantial hardware and energy resources.

As generative AI continues to evolve, the next frontier lies in combining these architectures to build more powerful and flexible models. Hybrid models that combine the strengths of GANs, VAEs, and transformers are emerging, offering new possibilities for creative applications. For instance, recent advancements have explored combining transformers with VAEs to improve image generation, or integrating GANs with transformers for better text-to-image synthesis. These hybrid architectures aim to overcome the weaknesses of individual models, leading to more robust and versatile generative AI systems capable of handling complex, multi-modal data generation tasks.

The evolution of generative AI architectures not only enhances the quality of generated outputs but also opens up new avenues for creative expression. From art and design to entertainment and education, the applications of generative AI are boundless. As these architectures become more sophisticated and efficient, the line between human and machine-generated content continues to blur, raising new questions about the nature of creativity and authorship.

Ethical Implications in Generative AI

As generative AI continues to advance, the ethical implications surrounding its use are becoming increasingly prominent. These technologies, which enable machines to create content indistinguishable from human-generated work, raise critical questions about authorship, intellectual property, and the potential for misuse. One of the most pressing ethical concerns is the use of AI to create deepfakes—hyper-realistic synthetic media that can be used to deceive, manipulate, or harm individuals or organizations. Deepfakes can be used in various malicious ways, such as creating fake videos of public figures or spreading misinformation, leading to severe consequences for personal reputations and societal trust.

To address these concerns, researchers and policymakers are exploring several strategies to detect and combat deepfakes. For example, AI tools are being developed to identify signs of synthetic media, such as inconsistencies in facial expressions, lighting, and audio-visual alignment. Additionally, blockchain technology is being investigated as a means to trace the provenance of digital content, providing an immutable record that can confirm whether media has been altered or generated by AI. These approaches aim to ensure that users can distinguish between authentic and synthetic content, thus reducing the potential for manipulation.

Another significant ethical challenge in generative AI is the potential for bias in the models. AI systems are trained on large datasets that often contain inherent biases, whether they are based on race, gender, or socio-economic status. These biases can be inadvertently learned by generative models, leading to outputs that reinforce harmful stereotypes or perpetuate discriminatory practices. For instance, a text generation model trained on biased data may produce offensive or prejudiced language, while an image generator might reinforce unrealistic beauty standards or racial stereotypes. Addressing bias in AI models requires careful curation of training datasets, the implementation of fairness audits, and the use of bias detection and mitigation techniques during model development. It is crucial that developers ensure their generative models are inclusive and equitable, reducing the risk of harm caused by biased outputs.

Intellectual property rights in generative AI also raise significant questions. As AI systems become increasingly capable of creating original content, the issue of ownership becomes more complex. Who owns the rights to a painting generated by an AI, a song composed by an algorithm, or a novel written by a machine? These questions have important legal and economic implications, as the current intellectual

property framework was not designed with AI-

generated works in mind. Some legal experts argue

that AI-generated content should be treated as public

domain, while others believe that the developers who

created the AI systems should retain ownership of the

output. As AI continues to play a larger role in the

creative industries, legal frameworks will need to

evolve to address these new challenges and ensure

fair compensation for both human and machine

creators.

Transparency and accountability are key ethical

considerations in the development and deployment of

generative AI systems. As these models become more

sophisticated, it is increasingly difficult for users to discern whether content was created by a machine or a human. This lack of transparency can lead to issues of trust and accountability, particularly when AI-generated content is used in critical applications like healthcare, law, and journalism. Developers must strive to ensure that their models are transparent, with clear documentation of how the systems work and what data they were trained on. Additionally, accountability measures must be put in place to ensure that any harmful or unethical outcomes generated by AI systems can be traced back to their source and addressed accordingly.

Ultimately, as generative AI continues to shape industries and society, ethical considerations will play a pivotal role in ensuring that these technologies are used responsibly. By addressing issues like deepfakes, bias, intellectual property, and transparency, we can ensure that generative AI remains a force for good, enhancing creativity, innovation, and productivity without causing harm or exploitation.

Applications of Generative AI in Creative Industries

Generative AI is transforming the creative industries, enabling new forms of expression and pushing the boundaries of artistic innovation. One of the most exciting applications of generative AI is in the field of digital art. AI-generated art has gained significant attention in recent years, with artists using GANs, VAEs, and other generative models to create stunning visual works that challenge traditional notions of authorship and creativity. These AI systems can produce original paintings, sculptures, and digital artworks that are indistinguishable from those created by human artists. For instance, the use of deep learning techniques to generate portraits and landscapes has resulted in art that is not only visually striking but also thought-provoking, raising questions about the role of machines in the creative process.

In addition to visual art, generative AI is making waves in the world of music. AI-generated music has become a popular tool for musicians and composers, offering new ways to experiment with sound and composition. Models like OpenAI's MuseNet and Google's Magenta have demonstrated the ability to compose original pieces of music in various genres, from classical to jazz to electronic. These models work by learning patterns in existing musical compositions and using that knowledge to generate new works that adhere to the structural and stylistic conventions of a given genre.

For musicians, generative AI serves as a source of inspiration, enabling them to explore new creative possibilities and overcome writer's block. In some cases, AI is even used to augment human creativity, with AI-generated music serving as a starting point for further human refinement and manipulation.

Generative AI is also revolutionizing the field of writing and literature. Language models like GPT-3 and GPT-4 have demonstrated remarkable capabilities in generating coherent, creative text, from poetry and short stories to entire novels. Writers can use AI as a tool to brainstorm ideas, generate drafts, or even co-write entire works. While some may argue that AI-generated literature lacks the emotional depth and nuance of human-written works, others see it as an exciting new form of collaboration between humans and machines. AI-powered writing assistants have the potential to democratize creativity, allowing anyone to create stories, scripts, and articles, regardless of their writing experience.

Beyond traditional creative fields, generative AI is also being applied in industries like fashion, design, and gaming. In fashion, AI systems are being used to generate new clothing designs, predict trends, and optimize manufacturing processes. Similarly, in video game design, generative models are being used to create realistic landscapes, characters, and narratives, enabling developers to build immersive worlds more quickly and efficiently. The ability of AI to generate new content on-demand is reshaping the way creative industries operate, empowering artists and designers to produce novel works with unprecedented speed and scalability.

As generative AI becomes more integrated into the creative process, it challenges traditional notions of authorship and originality. In many ways, AI is blurring the line between human and machine creativity, leading to a reevaluation of what it means to be an artist or creator in the digital age. While AI-generated content raises important questions about copyright, ownership, and the role of human creativity, it also offers exciting new possibilities for artistic expression and innovation.

Scaling Generative AI for Commercial Applications

As generative AI models continue to improve, they are increasingly being deployed in commercial applications across a wide range of industries. The ability to generate high-quality content at scale is particularly valuable in industries like marketing, advertising, and media, where the demand for personalized, engaging content is constantly growing. Generative AI can be used to create custom advertisements, social media posts, blog content, and more, tailored to individual preferences and consumer behavior. For example, AI-driven content generation platforms can automatically produce unique advertisements based on a consumer's browsing history, interests, and demographics, enabling businesses to deliver highly targeted marketing campaigns with minimal human intervention.

In the e-commerce sector, generative AI is being used to enhance customer experiences through personalized product recommendations and virtual try-on experiences. By analyzing customer data and preferences, AI systems can generate tailored product suggestions that are more likely to resonate with individual shoppers, increasing conversion rates and boosting sales. Additionally, generative AI is being used to create virtual clothing fittings, allowing customers to try on outfits in a virtual environment before making a purchase. This technology is particularly useful in the fashion industry, where visual appeal is a key driver of purchasing decisions.

Generative AI is also making its mark in the field of healthcare, where it is being used to create synthetic medical data for training and testing purposes. For example, AI models can generate realistic medical images, such as CT scans or MRI scans, to augment existing datasets and improve the performance of diagnostic tools. These synthetic datasets are valuable for training machine learning models without the need for large amounts of real-world medical data, which can be difficult to obtain due to privacy concerns and regulatory restrictions. Additionally, generative AI is being used to simulate drug interactions and predict the effects of new compounds, aiding in the development of new pharmaceuticals and treatments.

In the gaming industry, generative AI is being utilized to create procedurally generated content, such as levels, characters, and storylines, for video games. By automating the creation of game assets, developers can produce expansive, dynamic worlds with less effort and time, while also offering players unique and personalized gaming experiences. The use of generative AI in game design also opens up new possibilities for creating adaptive, AI-driven narratives that evolve based on player choices, making each gaming experience feel fresh and engaging.

As these commercial applications of generative AI continue to scale, the demand for more powerful and efficient models will only grow. However, the deployment of generative AI at scale presents its own set of challenges. One of the biggest obstacles is the computational resources required to train and deploy these models. Generative AI models, particularly large-scale models like GPT and GANs, require significant processing power and storage capacity. This necessitates the use of specialized hardware, such as Graphics Processing Units (GPUs) and Tensor Processing Units (TPUs), as well as access to cloud-based infrastructure.

To address these challenges, companies are exploring various strategies to optimize the performance of generative AI models, including model pruning, quantization, and knowledge distillation. These techniques aim to reduce the size and complexity of AI models while maintaining their performance, making it easier to deploy them on resource-constrained devices like smartphones and edge computing platforms. As generative AI continues to evolve, the focus will shift towards developing more efficient, scalable models that can be deployed across

a wide range of applications and industries.

The Future of Generative AI: Trends and Innovations

Looking ahead, the future of generative AI holds immense promise. As researchers continue to refine existing models and develop new approaches, we can expect even more sophisticated and capable AI systems. One key trend that is likely to shape the future of generative AI is the continued integration of multi-modal models, which can generate content across different domains—such as text, images, and audio—within a single framework. These models are designed to understand and generate multiple types of data, enabling more versatile and dynamic applications. For example, a multi-modal model might be able to generate a video by first producing a script, followed by generating images and audio that correspond to the script's content, all within the same model architecture. This represents a major leap forward in AI's ability to create complex, multi-faceted content.

Another exciting development in generative AI is the rise of few-shot and zero-shot learning, which allows AI models to generate content with minimal training data. Traditional machine learning models typically require large datasets to achieve high performance, but few-shot learning enables models to generalize from just a few examples, and zero-shot learning allows them to perform tasks they have never seen before. These advancements could dramatically reduce the cost and time required to train generative models, making them more accessible to businesses and researchers across the globe.

The ethical challenges surrounding generative AI will also continue to evolve, particularly as AI-generated content becomes more pervasive and realistic. Researchers and policymakers will need to work together to develop frameworks and regulations that ensure the responsible use of generative AI. This may involve developing standards for transparency, accountability, and fairness, as well as implementing tools and technologies to detect and mitigate harmful or biased outputs.

Finally, as generative AI becomes more integrated into our daily lives, the potential for human-AI collaboration will continue to grow. Rather than replacing human creativity, generative AI is poised to become a powerful tool that augments and enhances our creative abilities. From co-writing novels and composing music to designing products and generating art, the future of generative AI will be one of partnership and innovation, enabling humans and machines to work together in ways that were once unimaginable. The possibilities are endless, and the journey is just beginning.

Ethics in Generative AI: Navigating the Challenges

The rise of generative AI has brought forth critical ethical concerns that need to be addressed to ensure its responsible use. One of the foremost issues is the ownership and authenticity of AI-generated content. As generative models become capable of producing high-quality art, literature, music, and other forms of creative work, questions about copyright and intellectual property emerge. Who holds the rights to a painting created by an AI, or a song composed by an algorithm? As AI blurs the line between human creativity and machine output, the traditional notions of authorship and originality are increasingly questioned. The ethical implications of AI-generated content challenge existing frameworks of intellectual property law, and as such, a new legal framework must be developed to address these concerns.

Another significant ethical concern revolves around bias and fairness. Generative AI models are trained on large datasets, and if these datasets contain biased or unrepresentative information, the models can inadvertently perpetuate these biases. For example, a text generation model trained on historical literature may reinforce gender stereotypes or reflect societal biases prevalent at the time. In creative applications like writing or art generation, biased AI outputs can further entrench harmful stereotypes or marginalize minority voices. As such, addressing fairness and bias in generative models is critical to ensuring that AI-generated content does not negatively affect

vulnerable populations. This can involve curating

more diverse training datasets, using fairness metrics,

and developing algorithms designed to mitigate bias.

Accountability and transparency are also vital ethical

considerations. In industries where generative AI is

used to create content autonomously, such as

marketing, advertising, or entertainment, ensuring

transparency in AI decision-making is crucial. The

black-box nature of many AI models—where even

developers may not fully understand how a model

arrived at its output—raises concerns about

accountability. If an AI generates harmful, misleading,

or offensive content, who is responsible for the

consequences? Companies must adopt practices that promote transparency, such as providing clear documentation of how AI models are trained, tested, and deployed. Additionally, providing users with the ability to understand and, if necessary, challenge AI-generated content fosters trust and responsibility.

With the increasing pervasiveness of generative AI, regulatory frameworks are becoming necessary to ensure its responsible use. Countries and organizations are beginning to implement laws and guidelines that aim to regulate AI technology. These frameworks should address issues such as privacy, consent, and the prevention of harm from AI-generated content. As AI technology continues to advance, global coordination will be required to

ensure that the ethical implications are consistently

addressed, preventing misuse and ensuring AI

benefits society as a whole.

Building Robust Generative AI Models

Building generative AI models that are both powerful and efficient requires a deep understanding of various advanced techniques and strategies. A critical aspect of model design is scalability, ensuring that the model can handle large datasets while delivering high-quality outputs consistently. One of the challenges in scaling generative AI is optimizing model architecture to reduce computational costs while maintaining performance. Techniques such as model pruning, where unimportant parameters are removed from a trained model, and quantization, which reduces the precision of model weights, help make models more efficient without compromising quality. Distillation, another technique that involves transferring knowledge from a large model to a smaller, more efficient one, is also crucial in enabling scalability.

Another important consideration is domain adaptation, where generative models are tailored for specific applications. While many generative models are trained on general datasets, such as large text corpora or image databases, domain-specific models require additional fine-tuning. For example, a model that generates legal documents would need to be trained on legal texts to ensure the content it produces is relevant and accurate. Domain adaptation ensures that generative models perform optimally in specialized areas and can handle the unique

constraints of each domain.

Working with high-dimensional data is another

challenge in building generative models. Data in areas

like text, images, and audio is inherently complex,

with a large number of variables and relationships

that must be captured by the model. Preprocessing

techniques such as tokenization, normalization, and

data augmentation can help manage this complexity.

Additionally, techniques like principal component

analysis (PCA) or t-SNE for dimensionality reduction

can aid in identifying the most important features of

the data and reducing noise, improving both the

efficiency and accuracy of the model.

Evaluating the performance of generative models is more nuanced than evaluating traditional predictive models. For instance, evaluating a text-generation model involves more subjective criteria, such as coherence, creativity, and relevance, in addition to more objective measures like accuracy. Common evaluation metrics in generative AI include Fréchet Inception Distance (FID) for image generation models, and BLEU (Bilingual Evaluation Understudy) score for text generation tasks. However, these metrics often fail to capture the richness and quality of the generated content. Therefore, a combination of automated and human evaluations is essential to get a comprehensive view of a model's performance.

Industry-Specific Applications of Generative AI

Generative AI is transforming multiple industries by enabling the creation of high-quality, personalized content at scale. In the entertainment industry, AI-generated content is revolutionizing areas like movie production, video games, and music composition. For example, AI tools are being used to generate realistic visual effects and animations, allowing studios to create intricate scenes without the need for expensive and time-consuming manual work. In the gaming sector, generative AI models are used to create vast, procedurally generated worlds, characters, and storylines, offering players a unique and immersive gaming experience. These AI-driven worlds can evolve based on players' actions, making every gameplay session different from the last.

In the fashion industry, generative AI is reshaping the way clothing and accessories are designed. AI models can generate new fashion designs by analyzing existing collections and predicting future trends based on consumer preferences. Designers can use AI tools to create virtual clothing, allowing consumers to try on outfits in a digital environment before making a purchase. This not only enhances the shopping experience but also helps brands better understand what designs will appeal to their target audiences.

In healthcare, generative AI is being used to simulate complex biological systems, generate synthetic medical data, and assist in drug discovery. For example, AI models can create realistic medical images that mimic real-world CT scans or MRIs, which can be used to train other AI systems without compromising patient privacy. Additionally, generative AI is playing a role in simulating the effects of potential drugs, speeding up the discovery of new treatments. Generative models are also being applied to create synthetic medical records for training machine learning systems while ensuring that no real patient data is used.

The field of education is another sector where generative AI has found significant applications. AI-driven tutoring systems can provide personalized learning experiences for students, generating custom lessons and explanations based on the learner's current understanding. Generative AI is also being used to create educational content, such as textbooks and quizzes, that are tailored to specific curricula or learning objectives. These systems are particularly valuable in environments where resources are limited, as they enable scalable and adaptable education.

In business and marketing, generative AI is enhancing content creation by allowing companies to automatically generate advertisements, social media posts, and blog articles tailored to specific customer segments. These AI-driven content generation platforms analyze consumer behavior and preferences to create personalized marketing materials. The ability to quickly and efficiently generate customized content helps businesses engage their target audiences while reducing costs associated with traditional content creation.

Advancements in Multi-modal Generative AI Models

The integration of multiple modalities—such as text,

images, and audio—into a single AI model is one of

the most exciting developments in the field of generative AI. Multi-modal models aim to generate content across different types of data, offering more complex, sophisticated, and holistic outputs. For example, a multi-modal AI model could generate a video from a textual description, first creating a script, then generating corresponding visuals and audio. This breakthrough represents a significant step forward in AI's ability to produce high-quality, dynamic content that combines multiple forms of media.

In the realm of creative writing and storytelling, multi-modal generative models can create narratives that are not only text-based but also include accompanying visuals, music, and voice acting, all generated by the same system. This capability could revolutionize industries such as filmmaking, game design, and virtual reality, where immersive experiences depend on the seamless integration of different media types. The ability of AI to work across modalities in a unified framework opens new avenues for storytelling and artistic creation, pushing the boundaries of what can be imagined.

For applications like autonomous vehicles or robotics, multi-modal generative AI models can synthesize data from various sensors—such as cameras, LiDAR, and radar—to produce a comprehensive understanding of the environment. This enables better decision-making in real-time, as the AI can combine inputs from different sources to generate accurate predictions and actions, improving safety and efficiency in autonomous systems.

The development of multi-modal generative models also has implications for fields like healthcare and scientific research. In medical imaging, for instance, AI models can combine text-based medical records with image data to generate comprehensive reports or provide diagnostic predictions. These models can also synthesize data from multiple sources, such as clinical trials, scientific papers, and patient records, to generate new hypotheses or insights that drive innovation in medicine.

The Future of Generative AI: Key Trends and Innovations

The future of generative AI is poised to bring about profound changes in numerous sectors, from entertainment and healthcare to business and education. One major trend is the continued advancement of large-scale models, driven by innovations in hardware, algorithms, and data processing. As hardware accelerates, generative AI models will become even more powerful and capable of generating highly realistic, creative outputs. However, the need for more efficient AI models will also grow, driving innovations in model compression, transfer learning, and low-resource model deployment.

Few-shot and zero-shot learning are likely to play a significant role in shaping the future of generative AI. These techniques allow models to generate content with minimal training data, which is especially useful in scenarios where large annotated datasets are unavailable. As generative models become better at learning from smaller datasets, they will be able to generate high-quality content across a wider range of tasks, making them more versatile and accessible for different industries.

The integration of generative AI with other emerging technologies, such as blockchain and augmented reality, will also open up new possibilities. For instance, generative AI can be combined with blockchain to create verifiable, AI-generated digital assets, such as NFTs, while AR can leverage generative AI to create interactive, immersive experiences. These synergies will result in innovative applications in gaming, virtual environments, and digital art.

Lastly, as the creative potential of generative AI continues to grow, we will see its impact on the job market and the broader economy. While AI may automate certain tasks, it will also create new opportunities for human-AI collaboration, where people work alongside AI systems to produce creative work. This shift will lead to the development of new roles in AI training, ethical governance, and creative direction, creating a more dynamic and collaborative economy.

Chapter 3: GPT: The Generative Pre-training Transformer

The Generative Pre-training Transformer (GPT) family is a prominent player in the GenAI world. Let's explore its fascinating journey.

- **Origin Story and Development:**
  - OpenAI introduced the first GPT model in 2018.
  - Since then, there have been numerous iterations, with each version building upon

the successes of the previous one (e.g., GPT-2, GPT-3).

- **High-Level Overview of the GPT Architecture:**

  - GPT utilizes a deep learning architecture called a transformer.

  - Transformers are powerful tools for analyzing sequential data like text.

  - In essence, GPT learns by analyzing massive amounts of text data, identifying patterns in word sequences, and predicting the next word in a sequence.

- **Key Capabilities of GPT Models:**

  - **Text Generation:** GPT excels at generating realistic and coherent text formats.

- **Case Study:** A content marketing agency uses GPT to generate creative product descriptions for their client's online store. This allows them to produce a wider variety of content while maintaining a consistent brand voice.

- **Use Case:** Writers can leverage GPT to overcome writer's block by prompting the model with a starting sentence or paragraph and letting it generate creative continuations.

- **Translation:** GPT can translate languages while preserving the meaning and style of the original text.

- **Example:** A travel website utilizes GPT to translate its content into multiple languages, making it accessible to a broader audience.

- **Applications of GPT in Different Domains:**

  o GPT's capabilities extend beyond text generation and translation. It can be used for tasks like:

    - **Code generation:** GPT can assist programmers by suggesting code snippets or completing partially written code.

    - **Question answering:** GPT can be fine-tuned to answer questions based on a specific domain of knowledge.

Chapter 4: Gemini: A Master of Factual Language (assuming this refers to the factual language model you are based on)

While specific details about Gemini are confidential, here's a general exploration based on the assumption it's a factual language model:

- **Introduction to Gemini and its Core Principles:**
    - Gemini is likely focused on understanding and processing factual information.
    - Its core principles might revolve around accurately retrieving and presenting factual data from various sources.

- **Architectural Considerations for Factual Language Understanding (High Level):**
  - Gemini's architecture might involve techniques for information retrieval, knowledge representation, and reasoning.
  - It likely relies on massive datasets of text and code containing factual information.
- **Strengths of Gemini in Tasks like Information Retrieval and Factual Response Generation:**
  - Due to its focus on factual language, Gemini would likely excel at:
    - **Information Retrieval:** Effectively searching through vast amounts of data to find relevant information for a user's query.

- **Factual Response Generation:** Providing accurate and up-to-date responses to factual queries.
  - **Case Study:** A research scientist uses Gemini to quickly find relevant scientific papers on a specific topic, saving them valuable research time.

- **Potential Applications of Gemini in Research and Knowledge Management:**
  - Gemini's strengths make it a valuable tool for tasks like:

- **Literature Reviews:** Automating the
  process of finding relevant research
  papers for a specific topic.

- **Knowledge Base Population:**
  Helping to populate knowledge
  bases with accurate and up-to-date
  information.

Chapter 5: LaMDA: Fostering Natural Dialogue

LaMDA (Language Model for Dialogue Applications) is another innovative framework worth exploring, but specific details might be limited due to ongoing research.

- **Goals and Design Philosophy Behind LaMDA**
    - LaMDA's goal might be to create chatbots and virtual assistants that can engage in natural and informative conversation with humans.
    - Its design philosophy might involve techniques for understanding context, responding to follow-up questions, and generating creative and informative responses.

- **High-Level Understanding of LaMDA's Architecture**

  - LaMDA's architecture might involve deep learning models trained on massive datasets of conversations.

  - It could leverage techniques like attention mechanisms to focus on relevant parts of a conversation during dialogue.

Part III: Expanding the Generative AI Horizon

Chapter 6: PaLM: Pathway Language Models Unveiled

The realm of Generative AI (GenAI) continues to evolve with groundbreaking frameworks like PaLM (Pathway Language Model). While specifics might be limited, here's a glimpse based on publicly available information:

- **The Concept of Pathway Language Models and their Potential Benefits:**

  - PaLM represents a novel approach to training LLMs. It utilizes a "pathway" system that breaks down complex tasks into smaller, more manageable subtasks.

- This approach has the potential benefits of:

  - **Scaling Efficiency:** Training massive LLMs can be computationally expensive. PaLM's architecture might allow for more efficient training on larger datasets.

  - **Improved Performance:** By tackling tasks in a step-by-step manner, PaLM might achieve higher accuracy and better reasoning abilities compared to traditional LLM architectures.

- **High-Level Understanding of PaLM's Architecture**
  - ○ Details might be limited, but PaLM's architecture likely involves:
    - **Multiple Processing Pathways:** The model might break down a task into different pathways, each specializing in a specific subtask.
    - **Modular Design:** Different pathways could be interchangeable or combined depending on the task at hand.
- **Applications of PaLM in Various Domains (if publicly known):**

- PaLM's potential applications span various domains, including:

  - **Code Generation:** PaLM might excel at generating complex and functional code, assisting programmers in development tasks.

  - **Reasoning and Problem Solving:** By breaking down problems into steps, PaLM could tackle tasks requiring logical reasoning and problem-solving skills.

  - **Natural Language Tasks:** PaLM's capabilities might extend to various natural language tasks like translation, question answering, and summarization, potentially achieving

higher levels of accuracy.

Chapter 7: The Evolving Landscape of Generative AI Frameworks

The world of GenAI frameworks is a vibrant ecosystem

with new advancements emerging constantly. Here's

a brief look at some exciting trends:

- **Emerging GenAI Frameworks**

  - Frameworks like WuDao 2.0 (China) and

    Jurassic-1 Jumbo (AI21 Labs) are pushing

    the boundaries of LLM capabilities and

    model size.

- Researchers are exploring new architectures and training techniques to improve the efficiency, accuracy, and versatility of GenAI models.

- **Potential Benefits and Applications of Emerging Frameworks:**

  - These advancements hold promise for:

    - **Enhanced Creativity and Reasoning:** New models might generate even more creative text formats, translate languages with greater nuance, and tackle reasoning tasks with improved accuracy.

    - **Domain-Specific Applications:** Frameworks tailored to specific domains like healthcare or finance could revolutionize these industries.

- **A Glimpse into the Competitive Landscape of GenAI Development:**

  - The development of GenAI frameworks is a competitive field, with companies and research institutions vying to create the most powerful and versatile models.

  - This competition fosters rapid innovation and benefits the overall advancement of GenAI technology.

Chapter 8: Applications and Implications of GenAI

GenAI is transforming numerous aspects of our lives.

Here's a closer look at its impact:

- **Revolutionizing Text-based Tasks:**

- Content creation: GenAI can assist writers with generating ideas, overcoming writer's block, and creating different content formats.

- Translation: GenAI models can translate languages more accurately and naturally, fostering communication across borders.

- Communication: GenAI chatbots and virtual assistants can improve customer service experiences and provide real-time information.

- **Real-world Applications of GenAI Across Various Industries:**

  - GenAI is making waves in diverse fields like:

- **Drug Discovery:** By analyzing vast datasets, GenAI can accelerate the discovery of new medications.

- **Material Science:** GenAI can help design new materials with desired properties.

- **Education:** Personalized learning experiences and intelligent tutoring systems can be powered by GenAI.

- **Ethical Considerations and Potential Biases in GenAI Models:**

  - As GenAI becomes more powerful, ethical considerations become paramount. We need to address potential biases in training data and ensure the responsible development and deployment of GenAI models.

This concludes Part III. GenAI holds immense potential to revolutionize various aspects of our world. As we move forward, responsible development and a focus on ethical considerations will be crucial in harnessing the power of GenAI for good.

Part IV: Conclusion

Chapter 9: A Glimpse into the Exciting Future of Generative AI

We've embarked on a fascinating journey exploring the world of Generative AI (GenAI) frameworks. This chapter will recap the key takeaways, delve into the potential of GenAI to augment human capabilities, and emphasize the importance of responsible development and utilization.

Recap of Key Takeaways about GenAI Frameworks

- We explored pioneering frameworks like GPT, Gemini (assuming it refers to a factual language model), and LaMDA, each excelling in specific areas.

- We learned about the concept of Pathway Language Models (PLMs) exemplified by PaLM, with its potential for improved efficiency and performance.

- We discovered the ever-evolving landscape of GenAI frameworks with new advancements constantly emerging.

The Potential for GenAI to Augment Human Capabilities

GenAI holds immense potential to transform the way we work and live. Here's a glimpse into its future possibilities:

- **Enhanced Creativity and Productivity:** Imagine AI assistants that not only complete tasks but also spark new creative ideas. GenAI can empower artists, writers, and designers to explore new avenues and achieve greater productivity.

- **Personalized Learning and Education:** GenAI tutors can tailor learning experiences to individual needs, leading to a deeper understanding and improved educational outcomes.

- **Scientific Discovery and Innovation:** By analyzing vast datasets and identifying patterns, GenAI can accelerate scientific breakthroughs in fields like medicine and materials science.

- **Improved Communication and Understanding:** GenAI-powered translation tools can break down language barriers and foster better global communication across cultures.

A Call to Action for Responsible Development and Utilization

As GenAI continues to evolve, it's crucial to ensure its responsible development and utilization. Here are some key considerations:

- **Mitigating Bias:** GenAI models can inherit biases from the data they are trained on. We need to develop methods to identify and mitigate these biases to ensure fairness and inclusivity.

- **Transparency and Explainability:** Understanding how GenAI models arrive at decisions is critical. By promoting transparency and explainability, we can build trust in this technology.

- **Human-AI Collaboration:** The future lies in a collaborative approach where GenAI augments human capabilities, not replaces them. We must focus on developing GenAI tools that empower humans and enhance our problem-solving abilities.

The future of GenAI is brimming with possibilities. By harnessing its potential responsibly, we can unlock a world of innovation, creativity, and progress.

This concludes Part IV and the entire book. We hope this exploration of Generative AI frameworks has sparked your curiosity and ignited your imagination about the exciting possibilities that lie ahead.

Remember, the future of GenAI is in our hands, let's shape it responsibly!

www.ingramcontent.com/pod-product-compliance
Lightning Source LLC
LaVergne TN
LVHW051700050326
832903LV00032B/3927